Clarinet Cameos

Classic Concert Pieces

with

Orchestra

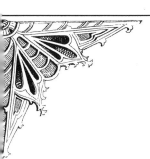

MMO

3259

SUGGESTIONS FOR USING THIS MMO EDITION

WE HAVE TRIED to create a product that will provide you an easy way to learn and perform concerted pieces with a full orchestra in the comfort of your own home. Because it involves a fixed orchestral performance, there is an inherent lack of flexibility in tempo. The following MMO features and techniques will reduce these inflexibilities and help you maximize the effectiveness of the MMO practice and performance system:

Where the soloist begins a piece or movement *solo*, we have provided an introductory measure with subtle taps inserted at the actual tempo before the soloist's entrance.

We have observed generally accepted tempi, but some may wish to perform at a different tempo, or to slow down or speed up the accompaniment for practice purposes. You can purchase from MMO specialized CD players & recorders that allow variable speed while maintaining proper pitch. This is an indispensable tool for the serious musician and you may wish to look into purchasing this useful piece of equipment for full enjoyment of all your MMO editions.

We want to provide you with the most useful practice and performance accompaniments possible. If you have any suggestions for improving the MMO system, please feel free to contact us. You can reach us by e-mail at *mmogroup@musicminusonecom*.

Music Minus One

3259

Clarinet Cameos

Classic Concert Pieces

WITH

Orchestra

COMPLETE VERSION TRACK	MINUS SOLOIST TRACK	SECTION	PAGE
	10	Tuning Notes: A440	
1	11	J.S. Bach: Air on a "G" String *(from the Orchestral Suite No. 3 in D major, BWV1068)*	5
2	12	Beethoven: Minuet in G *(arranged from the Minuet for Piano in G major, WoO10/2)*	6
3	13	Schumann: Träumerei *(arranged from 'Kinderszenen,' op. 15, no. 7)*	8
4	14	Schubert: Serenata *(adapted from 'Schwanengesang,' D957, no. 4: 'Ständchen')*	10
5	15	Raff: Cavatine, op. 85, no. 3	12
6	16	Mozart: Minuet *(arranged from Divertimento No. 17 in D major, KV320b (KV334))*	14
7	17	Godard: Berceuse *(arranged from the opera 'Jocelyn')*	16
8	18	Dvorák: Humoresque *(arranged from the Humoresque No. 7 for Piano, op. 101, no. 7)*	18
9	19	Brahms: Hungarian Dance No. 5 *(arranged from Hungarian Dance No. 5 for Piano Duet, WoO1/5)*	20

ISBN 1-59615-680-5

AIR ON A 'G STRING'

from the Orchestral Suite No. 3 in D major, BWV 1068

Johann Sebastian Bach
(1685-1750)

MINUET IN G

Ludwig van Beethoven
(1770-1827)
WoO 10/2

2 taps (²/3 measure)
precede music.

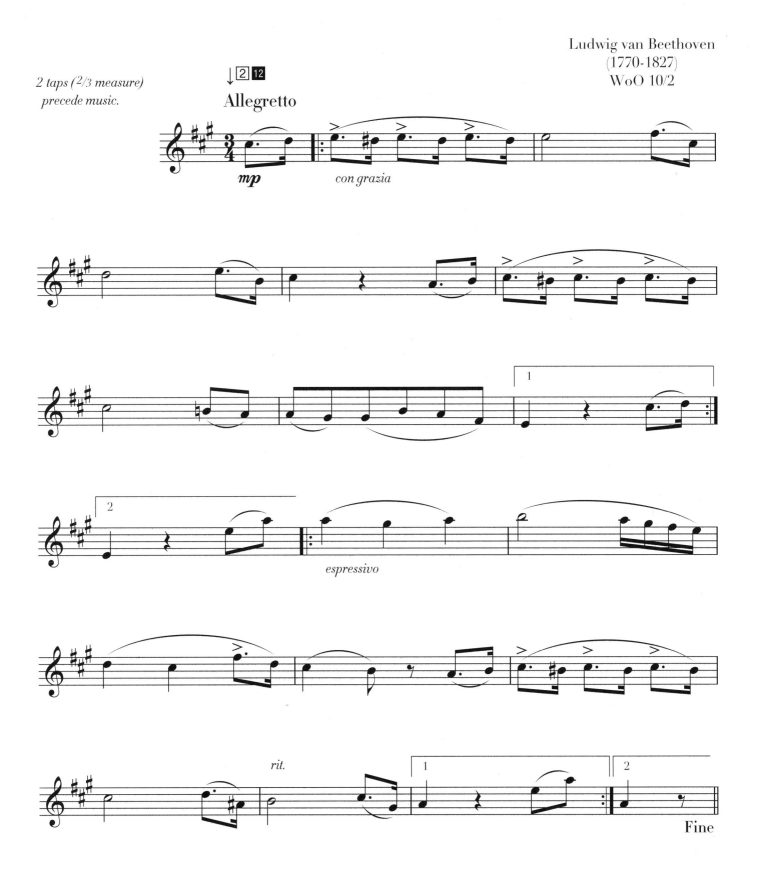

TRÄUMEREI

from Kinderszenen, op. 15

Robert Schumann
(1810-1856)

3 taps (¾ measure)
precede music.

Andante espressivo

SERENATA

adapted from Schwanengesang, D957, no. 4: *'Ständchen'*

Franz Schubert
(1797-1828)

CAVATINE
Op. 85, No.3

Josef Joachim Raff
(1822-1882)

*3 taps (¾ measure)
precede music.*

Larghetto, quasi Andantino

MINUET
from the Divertimento No. 17 in D, KV320b(KV334)

Wolfgang Amadeus Mozart
(1756-1791)

2 taps (²/3 measure)
precede music.

TRIO (slightly faster)

Menuetto D.C. al Fine

BERCEUSE
from "Jocelyn"

Benjamin Godard
(1849-1895)

HUMORESKE

Antonin Dvorák
(1841-1904)

Un più mosso

HUNGARIAN DANCE No.5

2 taps (1 measure)
precede music.

Johannes Brahms
(1833-1897)
WoO 1/5

Allegro

JUST A SAMPLING OF ALBUMS FOR

CLARINET

FROM MUSIC MINUS ONE

Clarinet in B-flat

Chamber Classics

BEETHOVEN Quintet for Piano and Winds in E-flat major, op. 16 MMO CD 3235

Harriet Wingreen, piano; New Art Wind Quintet: This quintet is Beethoven's at his best. One of the great classics of chamber music. The Andante is especially beautiful, with an almost perfect integration of all the instruments.

BRAHMS Clarinet Quintet in B minor, op. 115 (includes repitched B-flat version) MMO CD 3230

Collete Galante, clarinet - The Classic String Quartet: One of the summits of the chamber repertoire for clarinet, it is in many ways an homage to Mozart's classic quintet. Not to be overlooked by any serious clarinetist. Deluxe 2-CD set includes printed parts for both A and B-flat clarinets, plus a repitched version for B-flat clarinetists, allowing players of that instrument to learn the same fingerings as the composer's intended A clarinet for performance purposes. **(2CD Set)**

BRAHMS Sonatas in F minor and E-flat major, op. 120 MMO CD 3208

Jerome Bunke, clarinet - Hidemitsu Hayashi, piano: Favorites of clarinetists and pinnacles of the repertoire, these two sonatas are always popular on recital programs everywhere. Hear the piece performed by American virtuosoJerome Bunke, then you play them again with his accompanist. Presented here in the original key with printed parts for B-flat clarinets, this 2-CD set includes complete reference performance, piano accompaniments, plus a slow-tempo practice version of the accompaniments to help you as you learn the piece! **(2CD Set)**

MOZART Quintet for Piano and Winds in E-flat major, KV452 MMO CD 3236

Aldo Simonelli, clarinet - Harriet Wingreen, piano; New Art Wind Quintet: Mel Kaplan, oboe; Tina DiDario, bassoon; Murray Panitz, flute: Scored for piano, oboe, clarinet, horn and bassoon. Mozart's magnificent orchestration of the winds with piano creates a warm and glowing texture of sound. Each instrument emerges at times for a prominent position. Cast in three movements, it remains one of the great works in this format and wonderful fun to practice and perform.

MOZART Quintet in A major, KV581 (includes repitched B-flat version) MMO CD 3207

Keith Dwyer, clarinet - Cassini String Quartet: Charles Roth, 1st violin; Marla Smith, 2nd violin; John Madison, viola; John Iatzko, violoncello: Completed in September of 1789, this is one of Mozart's most perfect accomplishments--a score of proud serenity, transparent texture and radiant beauty. The solo clarinet leads the ensemble but does not subjugate it. There is an infinite variety of interplay between the performing partners, and all five instruments undertake the virtuoso's role at one time or another. 'The result,' says Homer Ulrich, 'is a piece of music whose charm and delicacy are difficult to duplicate in the literature of strings and winds.' Includes the quintet in its original key with printed parts for both A and B-flat clarinets, plus a repitched version for B-flat clarinetists. **(2CD Set)**

SCHUMANN Phantasiestücke, op. 73; 3 Romanzen (3 Romances), op. 94 MMO CD 3210

Jerome Bunke, clarinet - Hidemitsu Hayashi, piano: Pieces by the great Romantic master, Robert Schumann, which offer less experienced clarinetists a slice of nineteenth-century musical perfection. Highly recommended.

3 Romanzen, op. 94: *1. 'Nicht schnell'; 2. 'Einfach, innig'; 3. 'Nicht schnell';* Phantasiestücke, op. 73: *1. 'Zart und mit Ausdruck'; 2. 'Lebhaft, leicht'; 3. 'Rasch und mit Feuer'*

STRAVINSKY L'Histoire du Soldat (septet) MMO CD 3217

Robert Yamins, clarinet - Alice Poulson, violin; Glenn Rubin, bass; Harry Searing, bassoon; Gerald Kocher, trumpet; Sean Mahoney, trombone; James Preiss, percussion: Written in 1917 and one of the twentieth century's groundbreaking musical compositions. Stravinsky led the composing world with innovation and excitement. A work still widely performed in our time.

l'Histoire du Soldat: *The Soldier's March; Soldier at the Brook; Pastorale; The Royal March; The Little Concert; Three Dances (Tango, Waltz, Ragtime); The Devil's Dance; Grand Chorale; Triumphal March of the Devil*

WEBER Grand Duo Concertant; WAGNER Adagio MMO CD 3209

Jerome Bunke, clarinet - Hidemitsu Hayashi, piano: The Grand Duo Concertant is a magnificent piece for clarinet, displaying all the charm and rich woodwind character for which the composer was so justly famous; also included in this edition is a work by a man who was influenced profoundly by Weber: Richard Wagner's great Adagio.

Woodwind Quintets, vol. I Jewels for Woodwind Quintet MMO CD 3232

George Townsend, clarinet - Camerata Woodwind Quintet: Roy Lawrence, oboe; Gerald Carey, flute; Roger Collins, french horn; Robert Koper, bassoon: An eclectic assortment of pieces for woodwind quintet.

Barthe Passacaille: *Passacaille;* Beethoven *Quintet (adapted from sextet, op. 71);* Colomer *Bourée;* Haydn *Minuet; Rondo (Presto); Divertimento No. 1 in B-flat major, HobII/46;* Lefebvre Suite for Winds, op. 57: *II. Allegretto scherzando; III. Finale - Allegro leggiero;* Mozart *German Dance;* A. Reicha *Woodwind Suite in E-flat major*

Woodwind Quintets, vol. II Masterpieces for Woodwind Quintet MMO CD 3233

George Townsend, clarinet - Camerata Woodwind Quintet: Roy Lawrence, oboe; Gerald Carey, flute; Roger Collins, french horn; Robert Koper, bassoon: A varied and enchanting program of pieces for quintet by Bach, Haydn, Mozart, and others.

C.P.E. Bach *Andante (excerpt);* J.S. Bach Das Orgelbüchlein: *In Dulci Jubilo, BWV729 (chorale);* Balay *Petite Suite Miniature (I. Menuet; II. Courte Gavotte; III. Sarabande, IV. Petit Rondeau);* Colomer *Menuet;* Danzi *Quintet in G minor, op. 56, no. 2;* Deslandres Trois Pieces en Quintette: *Allegro;* Haydn *Introduction & Allegro for Woodwind Quintet (arranged from a piano trio in C major); Octet (Menuetto & Trio);* Klughardt Quintet, op. 79: *Andante grazioso;* Koepke *Rustic Holiday;* Mozart *Minuet, KV421;* Divertimento No. 14, V270: *Allegro molto;* Divertimento No. 8, KV213: *Andante & Contradanse*

Instrumental Classics with Orchestra

Art of the Solo Clarinet Orchestral Excerpts MMO CD 32

Laurence Liberson, clarinet - Stuttgart Symphony Orchestra/Emil Kahn: Famous clarinet excerpts from the classic repertoire. An opportunity to play these masterworks with a full orchestra. You function as 'soloist' as well as an integ member of the orchestra.

Beethoven Symphony No. 6, op. 68 'Pastoral' - Andante molto mosso, Andante con moto: *II. 'the brook-side'; 'By the brook-side' pt. 2;* Brahms *Haydn Variations;* Symphony No. 1 in C minor: *III. un po allegretto e grazioso (exerpt);* Mendelssohn Symphony No. 3 in A minor, op. 56 'Scottish': *I. Allegro un po agitato; II. Vivace non troppo;* Mozart Symphony No. 39 in E-flat major, KV543: *excerpt 1 (Andante con mot excerpt 2 (Menuetto);* Schubert *Marche Militaire;* Tchaikovsky 'Nutcracker' Suite, op. 71a: *Danse IV: 'Dan Arabe'; 'Waltz of the Flowers';* Wagner Siegfried Idyll, WWV103: *con moto (E major); Animato (E major)*

Band Aids Concert Band Favorites with Orchestra MMO CD 32

John Cipolla, clarinet - Stuttgart Festival Orchestra/Emil Kahn: A collection of classics spanning two centuries great music.

J.S. Bach *Chorale No. 42; Chorale No. 297;* Beethoven *Variations on a Theme by Paisiello; Contradanse;* The Ruin of Athens, op. 113: *Turkish March;* Brahms *A Melody Is Drifting;* Dvorak *Slavonic Dance;* D. Gabrielli Sacre Sym phoniae: *Canzon;* Haydn String Quartet in C major, 'Emperor,' op. 76, no. 3, HobIII/77: *II. Andant* Lully *Minuet;* Palestrina Te Deum Landamus (Mass): *Crucifixus;* Prokofiev The Love for Three Orange *March;* Smetana The Bartered Bride (Prodana Nevesta): *Polka;* Sullivan *There Lived a King;* Tchaikovsk Romeo and Juliet: *Theme;* Trad. (Hymn) *Christ the Lord Is Risen Today*

First Chair Clarinet Solos Orchestral Excerpts MMO CD 32

Laurence Liberson, clarinet - Stuttgart Symphony Orchestra/Emil Kahn: More excerpts from the symphonic repe toire displaying the clarinet's beauty. The player functions both as soloist and a member of the ensemble throughout th eclectic program. Any prospective first-chair clarinetist will find this training ground invaluable.

Beethoven *Country Dance No. 1; Country Dance No. 2; Country Dance No. 3;* Symphony No. 2 in D major, o 36 - Larghetto: *II. excerpt 1; excerpt 2;* Brahms Symphony No. 3 in F major, op. 90: *1st movement (excerpt 2nd movement (excerpt);* Mendelssohn Hebrides Overture, op. 26: *Fingal's Cave (excerpt);* Mozart *March No. KV408;* Schubert Symphony No. 8 in B minor 'Unfinished': *1st movement (excerpt); 2nd movement (excerpt* Tchaikovsky Symphony No. 5 in E minor, op. 64: *I. Andante - Allegro con anima (excerpt);* Weber Freischüt Der, J277: *Overture*

HAJDU Jewish Rhapsody for Clarinet/Bass Clarinet and Orchestra MMO CD 32

Orit Orbach, clarinet & bass clarinet - Plovdiv Philharmonic Orchestra/Nayden Todorov: This much-lauded concer by Israel's most heralded composer, Andre Hajdu, is set in movements alternating between B-flat clarinet and bas clarinet. Includes a version minus both instruments as well as one minus just B-flat clarinet for those who don't pla bass clarinet. A crowd-pleaser!

MOZART Concerto in A major, KV622 (New Recording - include repitched B-flat version) MMO CD 323

Denitza Lavchieva, clarinet - Tempi Concertati Chamber Orchestra/Nayden Todorov: Mozart did not make extensiv use of the clarinet until comparatively late in his career, but he wrote exquisitely for the instrument. The Concerto is i the conventional three movements, with music that transcends conventionality in its remarkable sense of repose an serenity, and what Bernhard Paumgartner has called 'its incredible warmth of tone, perfect balance and unmatche perfection of style.' It had a tremendous resurgence in popularity with the release of the Academy-Award-winning 198 film 'Out of Africa,' of which the piece formed a major element. In the original key with printed parts for both A and B-fla clarinets, plus a repitched version for B-flat clarinetists. **(2CD Set)**

Popular Concert Favorites with Orchestra MMO CD 324

John Cipolla, clarinet - Stuttgart Festival Orchestra/Emil Kahn: All-time standards arranged for clarinet and sym phony orchestra. A beautiful palette of sound. Not too difficult.

J.S. Bach *Sarabande;* Bizet Carmen: *Toreador Song;* Chopin *Prelude, op. 28, no. 7;* Dittersdorf *Tournament of Tem peraments (The Melancholic, The Humble, The Gentle);* MacDowell *To a Wild Rose;* Mendelssohn *Solemn March* Schubert *Moment Musical, op. 94, D780, no. 3;* Schumann Kinderszenen, op. 15: *7. Träumerei;* Verdi Aïda *Triumphal March*

SPOHR Concerto No. 1 in C minor, op. 26 MMO CD 320

Collete Galante, clarinet - Stuttgart Festival Orchestra/Emil Kahn: Ludwig Spohr, who created quite a stir when h began conducting with an odd contraption known as a baton, was also one of the best known violinists of his day, th first half of the nineteenth century. He is primarily known today for his concerti and other solo works for the fiddle. Tha he was also quite adept at writing for instruments other than his own is proved by this C-minor Clarinet Concerto, hi first of four such works, and a composition high on wit and solid craftsmanship. **(2CD Set)**

WEBER Concertino, op. 26, J109; BEETHOVEN Piano Trio No. 4, 'Street Song,' op. 11 MMO CD 320

Keith Dwyer, clarinet - Weber Concertino: Stuttgart Festival Orchestra/Emil Kahn; Beethoven Trio: Richar Mattson, violoncello; Robert Conway, piano: Carl Maria von Weber, great innovator and orchestrator who pave the way for such Romantic giants as Wagner and Liszt, wrote this famous and oft-performed "little concerto" in 1811 Lovely sonorities, beautiful themes—in short, a great piece for clarinet and orchestra. Also featured in this MMO edi tion, Beethoven's beautiful, warm-toned Piano Trio No. 4 is a treasure-trove of possibilities for the clarinetist. Lovel themes—young Beethoven at his best!

WEBER Concerto No. 1 in F minor, op. 73; STAMITZ Concerto No. 3 in B-flat major MMO CD 3202

Keith Dwyer, clarinet - Stuttgart Festival Orchestra/Emil Kahn: Carl Maria von Weber wrote several major works for Heinrich Joseph Baermann, one of the greatest clarinetists of the early nineteenth century. In his F-minor Concerto, it is clear that Weber knew the virtuosity of his player--he makes the soloist range over the entire compass of his instrument, and such quiet moments as do occur are invariably surrounded by runs, leaps and brilliant passagework. A fantastic concerto. Also in this edition is Carl Stamitz's B-flat-major concerto, a most beautiful Classical-era work. **(2CD Set)**

Student Series

Baermann Method, op. 63 The Virtuoso Clarinetist MMO CD 3240

John Cipolla, clarinet - piano accompaniment: A landmark recording of the entire Carl Baermann Method for Clarinet, the original and still most authoritative clarinet study. This first volume contains the complete opus 63 plus extensive notes on performance. Produced by John Cipolla, teacher, soloist and recitalist. A primary tool for teaching the clarinet—a master class! **(4CD Set)**

Baermann Method, op. 64 The Art of the Clarinet MMO CD 3241

John Cipolla, clarinet - keyboard accompaniment: The second half of MMO's classic recording of the entire Carl Baermann Method for Clarinet, the most revered and complete clarinet 'method' ever produced. Contains the complete opus 64 and extensive performance notes. Produced by John Cipolla, teacher, soloist and recitalist. **(4CD Set)**

Classic Themes *Student Editions, 27 Easy Songs - 2nd-4th year* MMO CD 3245

Harriet Wingreen, piano: Familiar world classics for clarinet and piano. Perfect for the intermediate player.

Albéniz *Tango;* Cohan Little Johnny Jones: *The Yankee Doodle Boy;* Curtis *Come Back to Sorrento;* Donato *A Media Luz;* Dvorak *Humoresque No. 7, op. 101, no. 7; Slavonic Dance;* Foster *Beautiful Dreamer;* Händel Xerxes (Serse), HWV40: *Largo;* Ivanovici *Waves of the Danube;* Key *The Star Spangled Banner;* Lehár *Gold and Silver (waltz);* Lemare *Andantino;* Leybach *Fifth Nocturne;* Offenbach *Apache Dance;* Les Contes d'Hoffmann (Tales of Hoffman): *Barcarolle (Moderato);* Pestalozza. *Ciribiribin;* Rubinstein *Melody in F, op. 3, no. 1;* Schubert *Moment Musical;* Ellens Gesang III: *'Ave Maria', op. 52, no. 6;* J. Strauss, Jr. *Blue Danube (waltz); Tales from the Vienna Woods;* Tchaikovsky *None but the Lonely Heart (Nur wer die Sehnsucht kennt), op. 6, no. 6;* Trad. (English folk song) *Country Gardens (English folk song);* Trad. (Gypsy melody) *Two Guitars;* Trad. (Gypsy song) *Dark Eyes;* Trad. (Scottish song) *Loch Lomond;* Wagner Tannhäuser, WWV70: *Evening Star*

Easy Clarinet Solos, vol. I - Student Level MMO CD 3211

Harriet Wingreen, piano: Pieces for the beginning clarinetist. Suitable for first through third year of study.

Stephen Adams *The Holy City;* Beethoven *Für Elise;* di Capua *'O Sole Mio!;* Chiara *La Spagnola;* Chopin *Fantaisie Impromptu, op. 66 (theme);* Clay *I'll Sing Thee Songs of Araby;* Crouch *Kathleen Mavourneen;* Dacre *Daisy Bell (A Bicycle Built for Two);* d'Hardelot *Because;* Elgar *Pomp and Circumstance;* Fearis *Beautiful Isle of Somewhere;* Flotow Martha: *'Ah, So Pure' ('Ach, so Fromm');* Geibel *Kentucky Babe;* Grieg *Main Theme;* Harris *After the Ball;* Herbert *Serenade;* The Fortune Teller: *Gypsy Love Song;* Howe *Battle Hymn of the Republic;* Jacobs-Bond *I Love You Truly;* Jacobs-Bond (m); Stanton (l) *Just A-wearyin' for You;* Koven *O Promise Me;* Lehár Die Lustige Witwe (The Merry Widow): *'Vilja';* Lincke *The Glow Worm;* MacDowell *To a Wild Rose;* Meacham *American Patrol;* Nevin *Mighty Lak' a Rose; The Rosary;* Nugent *Sweet Rosie O'Grady;* Partichella *Mexican Hat Dance;* Rachmaninov *Piano Concerto No. 2 in C minor, op. 18 (Theme);* Rimsky-Korsakov *Song of India;* Rodrigues *La Cumparsita;* C. Sanders *Adios Muchachos;* Schubert *Who Is Sylvia?;* Sibelius *Finlandia;* Tchaikovsky *Marche Slave;* Trad. (American cowboy song) *Red River Valley;* Trad. (Hebrew melody) *Eili, Eili;* Trad. (Hebrew national anthem) *Hatikvoh (The Hope);* Trad. (Neapolitan song) *Santa Lucia;* Trotère *In Old Madrid;* Villoldo *El Choclo;* Ward, Charles E. *The Band Played On;* Ward, Samuel A. (m); Bates, Katharine Lee (l) *America, the Beautiful;* Yradier (Iradier) *La Paloma*

Easy Clarinet Solos, vol. II - Student Level MMO CD 3212

Harriet Wingreen, piano: Volume Two is drawn from traditional and classical repertoire for clarinet and piano. Suitable for first-year through third-year students, this album will make practicing a true joy!

Jay Arnold *Blues in E-flat;* J.S. Bach *Jesu, Joy of Man's Desiring; Chorale No. 83;* Das Orgelbüchlein: *In Dulci Jubilo, BWV729 (chorale);* Bizet Carmen: *Toreador Song;* Borodin Prince Igor: *Melody (Moderato);* Brahms *Cradle Song;* Daniels *You Tell Me Your Dream;* Eastburn *Little Brown Jug;* Howard & Emerson *Hello! My Baby;* Lawlor The Sidewalks of New York: *The Sidewalks of New York;* Mendelssohn *Nocturne;* Offenbach *Bluebeard (scene);* Prokofiev *Peter and the Wolf, op. 67;* Rimsky-Korsakov *The Young Prince and the Young Princess; Sheherazade, op. 35;* Schubert *Valse Noble, op. 77, D969;* Smetana *The Moldau (theme);* Sousa *The High School Cadets; Manhattan Beach; The Rifle Regiment; The Stars & Stripes Forever;* J. Strauss, Jr. Der Zigeunerbaron (The Gypsy Baron): *Recruiting Song;* Josef Strauss *Fireproof Polka;* Stravinsky l'Oiseau de Feu (The Firebird): *Berceuse;* Sullivan H.M.S. Pinafore: *excerpt;* Thompson *Far Above Cayuga's Waters;* Trad. *I Ain't Gonna Study War No More; On Top of Old Smoky; Mr. Frog Went a'Courtin'!; When I Was Single; Old Paint; Careless Love; When the Saints Go Marching In;* Trad. (college song) *Spanish Guitar;* Trad. (English folk song) *Greensleeves;* Trad. (Folk song) *Black Is the Color of My True Love's Hair;* Trad. (Russian folk song) *The Cossack*

Take a Chorus B-flat/E-flat Instruments MMO CD 7008

Ed Xiques, baritone, tenor, alto and soprano saxophone - Stan Getz, tenor sax; Hal McKusick, clarinet & flute; Jimmy Raney, guitar; George Duvivier, bass; Ed Shaughnessy, drums: Designed to give the student player valuable practice in the area of ensemble playing, as well as improvising. Also of interest to the professional, who can use it for enjoyment and practice. All ten arrangements have the instrumental parts included with example solos on each tune in smaller notes to serve as a guide.

Fools Rush In; I've Got It Bad and That Ain't Good; Just You, Just Me; How About You?; Sunday; Beta Minus; Jupiter; Spring Is Here; Darn that Dream; This Heart of Mine

Teacher's Partner *Basic Clarinet Studies for the Beginner* MMO CD 3231

Scales in varied articulations, solos and duets with piano accompaniment. Covers first year of study and can be used with any method book. Addresses problems of pitch, rhythm, tone and articulation, presenting a professional model.

B-Flat Clarinet Tuning Instructions; G-major scale (using whole notes; then using quarter notes; then using half notes); F-major scale (using dotted half notes; then quarter notes; then using half notes followed by quarter notes); A-major scale (using half notes; then quarter-note/quarter-rest alternations; then using eighth notes); B-flat major scale (using half, quarter and two eighth notes; then using a quarter followed by two eighths; then using a dotted quarter followed by an eighth); C-major scale (using whole notes; then sixteenth notes); D-major scale (using dotted whole notes; then quarter-sixteenth note combinations); Scale Cycle (6 scales); Solo in G major; Perky Piggies (duet in G major); Dream Waltz (solo in F major); Two in Three (duet in F major); March of the Toys (solo in A major); Graceful Partners (duet in A major); Romance (solo in B-flat major); Canon in B-flat major; Banjo Song (solo in C major); Igorcentric (duet in C major); Peaceful Scene (duet in D major); Blueper (duet in B minor); Graduation Piece for B-flat clarinet

Twelve Classic Jazz Standards *B-flat/E-flat/Bass Clef Parts* MMO CD 7010

Bryan Shaw, trumpet - The MMO All-Star Rhythm Section: These historic recordings of standards were made at Judson Hall in Manhattan in 1951 and feature, literally, legends in jazz. Beautiful renditions of some of the finest songs of the 20th century. These backgrounds feature accompaniments by such players as Nat Pierce and Don Abney (piano); Barry Galbraith and Jimmy Raney (guitar); Milt Hinton and Oscar Pettiford (bass); and Osie Johnson and Kenny Clarke (drums). Classic recordings! Includes sheet music for E-flat, B-flat and Bass Clef instruments. The pristine digital transfers of the original recordings put you right there with these jazz immortals! **(2CD Set)**

April in Paris; I Got Rhythm; Oh, Lady Be Good; Embraceable You; Porgy and Bess: *The Man I Love; Body and Soul; Poor Butterfly; Three Little Words; What Is This Thing Called Love?; Lover Come Back to Me; I Only Have Eyes for You; Sometimes I'm Happy*

Twelve More Classic Jazz Standards *B-flat/E-flat/Bass Clef Parts* MMOCD7011

Tom Fischer, alto/tenor sax - The MMO All-Star Rhythm Section: This second album of historic recordings continues with a fabulous collection of standards. Your backgrounds for these classics are created by legends Don Abney (piano); Mundell Lowe and Jimmy Raney (guitar); Oscar Pettiford and Wilbur Ware (bass); and Kenny Clarke and Bobby Donaldson (drums). Includes sheet music for E-flat, B-flat and Bass Clef instruments. A true time machine to the greatest days of jazz accompaniments, in digitally remastered sound. **(2CD Set)**

You Go to My Head; Strike Up the Band; I Cover the Waterfront; Too Marvelous for Words; Crazy Rhythm; Don't Take Your Love From Me; Just One of Those Things; My Heart Stood Still; I May Be Wrong (But I Think You're Wonderful) [from the 1929 revue]; When Your Lover Has Gone; Fine and Dandy; Jeepers Creepers

World Favorites *Student Editions, 41 Easy Selections (1st-3rd year)* MMO CD 3244

Harriet Wingreen, piano: The New York Philharmonic's legendary pianist, Harriet Wingreen, accompanies you in forty-one selections from around the world, chosen for their beauty and ease of performance. Certain to delight the beginning student.

Balfe *Then You'll Remember Me;* Becucci *Tesoro Mio;* di Capua *'O Sole Mio!;* Chopin *Etude, op. 10, no. 3;* Daly *Chicken Reel;* Debussy *Clair de Lune;* d'Hardelot *Because;* Dresser *On the Banks of the Wabash;* Evans *In the Good Old Summertime;* Franck Messe solennelle, op. 12, M61: *5. Panis Angelicus (O Lord Most Holy);* Gruber *Silent Night;* Herbert *Romany Life;* J.H. Hopkins *We Three Kings of Orient Are;* Jessel *Parade of the Tin Soldiers;* Kennedy *Star of the East;* Lehár Die Lustige Witwe (The Merry Widow): *The Merry Widow Waltz;* Lincke *The Glow Worm;* MacDowell *To a Wild Rose; To a Water Lily;* Marchetti *Fascination;* L. Mason *Nearer, My God, to Thee;* Mendelssohn *Hark, the Herald Angels Sing;* Murray *Away in a Manger/Silent Night;* Neidlinger, W.H. *The Birthday of a King;* Nevin *Mighty Lak' a Rose;* Olcott *My Wild Irish Rose;* Poulton *Aura Lee;* Reading *Come All Ye Faithful;* Spilman *Flow Gently, Sweet Afton;* Trad. *He's Got the Whole World in His Hands;* Trad. (American cowboy song) *The Yellow Rose of Texas; Red River Valley;* Trad. (English folk song) *Greensleeves;* Trad. (Folk song) *Black Is the Color of My True Love's Hair;* Trad. (Irish melody) *Londonderry Air;* Trad. (Irish song) *Sweet Molly Malone;* Trad. (Scottish song) *Blue Bells of Scotland;* Trad. (Spiritual) *Deep River;* Trad. (U.S. Army Song) *Caisson Song;* Trad. (U.S. Marine Corps Song) *The Marines' Hymn;* Trad. (Welsh song) *All through the Night;* Yradier (Iradier) *La Paloma*

For our full catalogue of clarinet releases, including more popular and jazz titles, classical concerti, chamber works and master classes visit us on the web at

www.musicminusone.com

Call 1-800 669-7464 in the USA • 914 592-1188 International • Fax: 914 592-2751
email: mmogroup@musicminusone.com

MUSIC MINUS ONE
50 Executive Boulevard
Elmsford, New York 10523-1325
800-669-7464 (U.S.)/914-592-1188 (International)

www.musicminusone.com
e-mail: mmogroup@musicminusone.com